Just
Another
Senior
Surprise

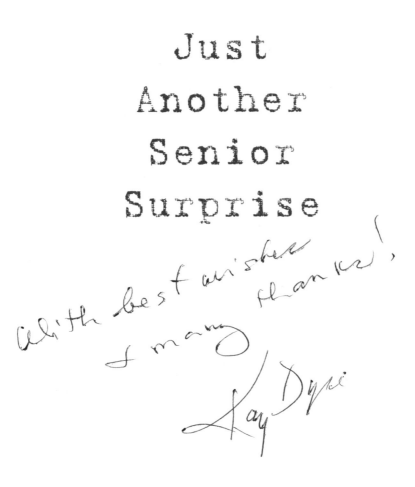

With best wishes
& many thanks!

Kay Dyke

Just
Another
Senior
Surprise

A Treatise on Aging

Reflections &
Observations by

KAY DYRE

Cover photo © David Stork
www.dstorkphoto.com

Just Another Senior Surprise: A Treatise on Aging

Print ISBN: 9798489788762

Copyright © 2021 by Kay Dyre.

Text design: Preferred Printing, Sioux Falls SD

Dedication

This book is dedicated
in memory of Evelyn,
who shared it all.

Acknowledgments

One of the proudest and happiest days of my life was the day I read a whole book all by myself. I was five years old. The book was short. I was hooked for life. No wonder I began to dream of writing a book of my own.

Just Another Senior Surprise is the answer to my dream. It came about through the kindness and generosity of Bob and Mary Boerigter, self-published friends. Marti Leishman had read my manuscript and referred it to them. Dave Stork provided the photo for the cover. All are friends and long-time guests at our family business, Evergreen Lodge. It was a team effort, but the Boerigters carried the load to completion.

My gratitude to all of them is indescribable and humble, and well deserved.

Table of Contents

Introduction

Introduction

Everyone over 60 knows about the "Senior Moment." It's that space in time when the word you are trying to think of or say just disappears into the air or shimmers outside your grasp for a short time, then suddenly pops back into focus before you can say "Shazam," or maybe some other S-word.

Being aware of this puzzlement is a good thing. It prepares you for the subject I am here to share, especially with anyone over 60, the ones it should concern. And frankly, it will.

I speak of the "Senior Surprise." My own discovery of, and experience with this phenomenon are herewith documented for your enlightenment, and as a fair warning.

Fear not. All shall be revealed in a timely manner.

Read carefully; consider fully.

You can thank me later.

Kay Dyre
Evergreen Lodge
Park Rapids, Minnesota
July 2021

Chapter 1

Revelation

It all started in June 2008, my 75th year. This was the month I received letters from my doctor, my dentist and my attorney all telling me that they would be retiring at the end of the year.

"And what" I said to myself, "is wrong with this picture?"

First of all, they were all younger than me.

Secondly, they had all been carefully chosen and tested and proven satisfactory, so I had no need or desire to change them.

Thirdly, many others in these professions locally were perhaps too young and inexperienced to meet my needs.

It was here I began to realize that life as a senior citizen would be a whole new reality that would be filled with many senior surprises, ready or not.

Since then, I have been abandoned by three more doctors, another dentist, my ophthalmologist, my accountant and my 37th paper boy.

So, there you have it. My life is totally out of control and there is nothing I can do about it. But I'm keeping my eye on the only undertaker.

Chapter 2

Senior Moments

Do you ever get upset with yourself when you have a senior moment? Well, don't! When you think of the information that has been stuffed in our brains over a lifetime, it is no wonder some of it gets lost from time to time.

Much of what we lose is no longer important anyway. What does it matter if Aunt Sally's 2nd husband's name was Roy or Ray, or even Roger? Why worry about some historic date that you can quick check with your computer? When was the last time you needed to be aware of "Pi" unless you had a scoop of ice cream to put on it? It was school that filled our heads with too much information. Not our fault at all.

Since then, my brain has become more resistant or maybe less able. Whatever the case, I find a lot of the things we are presented with just do not "stick." Some of it clearly clashes. For example, in my time, "Spam" was what we ate for lunch, preferably on rye with lettuce and mayonnaise. "Mail" was delivered by people, not machines. And "Homeland Security" was the old black lab named Pal.

Some old learning stays with us, of course. Tripping on

that old throw rug and breaking your arm will remind you that you have 205 bones to go. Hooking your hearing aids, glasses and oxygen hose over your ears will explain why cartilage grows forever.

I seem to remember what I really need to. That's good enough for me.

Chapter 3

Fashionista

I have never been known as a fashionista, but I know a lady must make an effort to at least look appropriate for the occasion, whatever that may be.

When your social life is limited to church doings, occasional lunch with friends, and too frequent funerals, your wardrobe could become outdated or even frumpy. That old navy-blue suit is still that old navy-blue suit, no matter how many different blouses, scarves, vests and necklaces you throw on it.

So go shopping.

I had, through observation over the years, determined that fashion designers are forbidden to ever look at any female body over 40. How can you design for wider hips, innertube waistlines or bountiful but sagging bosoms if you have never seen any?

You can't, and they don't.

Nevertheless, I was in desperate need of an outfit for a summer wedding. I grabbed a close friend and off we went to the mall. The women's wear was arranged into misses, juniors and seniors' departments, with sub-choices of formal, casual

5

or sportswear.

By then I was somewhat confused, but it was the "reduced price seasonals" and "close-out specials," plus "2 for 1" sales and coupon deals or credit card discounts that had me on the ropes. I leaned on the counter of the perfume section, hoping a squirt of some exotic fragrance would clear my head and set me back on course.

It looked like that had done the trick until I encountered an alcove dedicated to the Extra-Large Petite. The vision created in my over-loaded mind was one that provoked the loudest and most hysterical laughter ever to echo the hallowed halls of J.C. Penney.

I believe that being abruptly hustled from the store by a very red-faced friend could qualify as just another Senior Surprise.

Chapter 4

The "D" Dilemma

Some senior surprises are more worrisome than others. For some the worst of all is the senior "diaper dilemma."

What a nasty, insulting, demeaning and embarrassing – not to mention expensive – problem that is!

Where to buy them so one sees you? What size, shape or brand is the best? How often to change them? How to fit one in a purse or pocket? How to dispose of them in public?

Don't scoff. Your turn could come. Depend on it.

And you know what? After you've done your research, found out which one is best for you, put one on under your favorite party dress and headed out for the evening with friends, the only thing you will feel about the diapers is gratitude.

Now that's a <u>real</u> Senior Surprise.

Just Another Senior Surprise

Chapter 5

Say What?

Not all Senior Surprises are created equal. Some are shocking, some are funny, and some are simply mystifying.

At some point in your life you will start to notice that everyone around you has suddenly been struck with vocal anomalies that are annoying, confusing, and just plain unintelligible.

There will be the mumblers, the mutterers, the whisperers and the machine-gunners, none of which makes communication likely. As a result, your own speech will be reduced to a series of "What did you say?", "Say again, please?", or "Could you speak up a bit?"

What is the matter with these people? How can they not be aware of their problem? It is truly bizarre, plus seemingly incurable, despite all your efforts at correction. They simply do not hear you.

My personal experience with this problem led me to bring it up with my Doctor, a very wise and capable gentleman I trust implicitly. I knew he'd have the answer and solution.

He did.

Thus mystifying moments became a Senior Surprise

number 3, followed by a trip to Hearing Aid Haven for testing and fitting.

It was amazing how that simple test cured so many people.

Chapter 6

Driving

The one thing that seniors seem to dread most is losing their right to drive. Me too. I swore I would fight them to the finish to be able to keep my wheels rolling independently. Or so I thought.

I was sitting in a large parking area waiting for a friend when I finally "got it." At that moment I suddenly realized just how many older drivers there really are and just what a hazard they can be.

They were all there. Drivers leaning on canes. Drivers struggling with walkers. Drivers with obvious vision and hearing problems. Drivers who couldn't see over the steering wheel or reach the pedals. Drivers seemingly on their own private road, totally unaware of any other traffic. Drivers who didn't use turn signals or left them on too long. Drivers who blithely ignored speed limits. I had not seen anything so scary since I was a four-year-old and the neighbor's son dressed up like Frankenstein's monster for Halloween!

I thought about all this as I carefully drove home later. When I arrived at home, I hung the car keys on the hook by the door, as always. They should be easy to find when my family decides my driving days are done. It was the right thing to do, which made for just one more Senior Surprise.

Chapter 7

The Nose Knows

I really don't mind <u>being</u> an old lady. I also don't mind <u>looking</u> like an old lady. And most days I can handle <u>feeling</u> like an old lady. But I really, really HATE <u>smelling</u> like an old lady!

You cannot avoid it. When your heart and lungs are functioning at 70% or less capacity, every effort makes you sweat. And sweat stinks.

With taste buds that have bloomed and are dying out, the cravings for more flavor lead to dubious choices. Pickles, olives, sauerkraut and onions all add a lot to a dreary sandwich, but even more to a roiling gut. That leads to a 2-fer: bad breath <u>and</u> gassy gut.

Personal hygiene can take a beating, too. If you live alone, those showers taken with one hand in a death grip on the safety bar and the other trying to juggle the washcloth and slippery bar of soap to swab off your droopy hide, the results may not be as you'd prefer.

But worst of all is the endless lingering odor of pee. That was what sent me on the search for a cure, so to speak.

I headed to the drugstore to see what might be available to solve this problem. Several different styles and types of senior "underpants" were neatly lined up on the shelves. And sure enough, I spotted a product that was not only lavender scented, but also cheaper. Another 2-fer. How could I lose?

I hurried home, eager and hopeful. I set my purchase on the table, quickly taking out the package and opening it. My cat, asleep on his chair in the sunshine, immediately sat up, sniffed the air, nose and whiskers twitching and tail snapping, and headed for the door! How was I to know that cats don't like lavender?

I had to admit that once opened, the lavender really packed a wallop. In no time my eyes and nose were running and my lungs burning. What had I gotten into?

As a child of the Depression and the rationing of World War II, there was no option of throwing the underpants away. There must be a way to salvage them. Perhaps a good airing was the answer.

So, there I was, clothespins and flashlight in hand, at 9 o'clock at night, hanging eleven lavender drenched diapers on the clothesline. Unbelievable. I just wished someone had told me it might rain.

I'm a light sleeper and just happened to hear the first raindrops hit my window. I had just enough time to dash outside and rescue the panties from the line. Only I got wet.

I spread the panties around the basement floor to dry out and went back to bed, my hands smelling and my nose running.

Luckily all was not a total loss. The airing had helped

and I decided I could use one now and then. But the basement will never be the same. Somehow, I cannot recommend musty lavender as a room deodorizer.

The cat totally agrees.

Chapter 8

Chicken!

Becoming a senior citizen was really not much of a surprise. It was more of an inevitability. I expected wrinkles, droops and sags. I knew there would be slow downs and can't dos. I figured on ACHES AND PAINS. But I never expected to turn "chicken!"

That status arrived slowly and was usually prompted by some minor shock or upset. Maybe it was losing the car keys. Not me, you think? Until you do. You won't forget that day.

The first time another driver gives you a nasty horn blast, or even the finger, you'll wonder "What did I do?" or "Is it time for me to give up driving?"

Just how can the house you've lived in for forty-years suddenly develop moans and groans and loud thumps in the night none of which you've ever noticed before?

This sudden awareness leads to new fearfulness that can change the bravest of us into Rhode Island Reds, Grandma's favorite chickens.

Once the downhill slide is on full avalanche setting, all you can do is ride it out. The term "scared witless" had a whole new meaning.

Locking doors, leaving on lights, turning up the TV were my first lines of defense at home. Being outside was even harder. Traffic scared me, shopping intimidated me, just getting around seemed to freeze me in place.

What's a mother to do, indeed! I'm working on that. Meanwhile, all I can say for sure is "Cluck, cluck, cluck." And you can quote me.

Chapter 9

Urge to Purge

I have never been, nor cared to be, known as an "Immaculate Housekeeper." My own mother once gave me a metal plaque that reads:

MY HOUSE IS CLEAN ENOUGH TO BE HEALTHY
AND DIRTY ENOUGH TO BE HAPPY.

I'm still not sure how to take that, but it proudly hangs on my kitchen wall next to the one I made in a craft class. IT says:

EAT OFF THIS FLOOR
At Your Own Risk!

I have nothing against "clean" or "spotless." I just decided there had to be more to life than rearranging dust every day.

When I got to "Senior" status, a surprising thing happened. Every now and then I get this "urge to purge." It can happen at any time and nothing is safe or sacred.

Old books, old clothes, and old household items that are no longer used are promptly "culled from the herd," so to

19

speak. Most can be put to good use yet, and new gathering places are soon found for all.

After day of rest, I moved into Phase 2, the clothes closets. Their contents filled several more bags with items for the Thrift Shop. Phase 3 I dedicated to cleaning out drawers, which mostly produced garbage. There is just no demand for empty toothpaste tubes or dried out face creams.

Almost anything can trigger one of these spells. Recently I opened the hall closet door to throw some dirty clothes in a box I keep there to collect them. The box was overflowing and so was the whole closet!

My duty was clear. I spent three days sorting it all out, but at the end I had six big bags of recyclables and the cleanest closet in town. I found a taker for every single bag.

After a day of rest, I moved into Phase 2, the clothes closets. Their contents filled several more bags with items for the Thrift Shop. Phase 3 I dedicated to cleaning out drawers, which mostly produced garbage. There is just no demand for empty toothpaste tubes or dried out face creams.

The worst of all was Phase 4, the kitchen cupboards. Cans marked "Use by 2006" or spices dated 1997 were immediately tossed. Tomato-stained plastic containers with 37 non-fitting lids went next. Handfuls of expired coupons were shown no mercy. Dozens of twist-ties and cracker crumbs, moldy bread crusts, fossilized cookies, old raisins and wrinkled napkins were promptly disposed of. It was time for a break.

The final assault was on the refrigerator, and it also produced only garbage. A petrified orange, 2 rotten apples and a frozen head of lettuce went first. Freezer dried chicken thighs, a crumbling pizza and old biscuit dough also made the list. The final item turned out to be a carton of shriveled-up old ice cream that even the cat wouldn't touch. I hauled out so much garbage and trash I figured the garbage man would think

I was moving out!

It had all been a good start but many items still remained. Who would get the bronzed baby shoes with picture frame? Or the family albums? Or Grandma's hand-made quilts? Or the chest of party silverware? It would all just have to wait for the next "urge to purge".

A woman's work IS never done, and that's no surprise to anyone.

Chapter 10

Reality Check

Senior surprises come in all shapes and sizes, and all threat
levels. Some are just annoying, others quite scary. It's all in
your own point of view.

A good friend was recently widowed. A very capable
and hard-working lady, she had cared for her husband through
his long illness, taking on all chores every day. After he died,
she just continued the chores alone.

That worked for a while, then when the second Fall
rolled around, she just started the usual outdoor clean up.
Flower beds were cleaned out, the garden winterized, and leaf
raking and hauling began. It was the raking that finally did her
in.

She woke up the second morning with aches and pains
she could not believe. Stiff back, sore arm and leg muscles, leg
cramps and aching hands all assailed her.

It took three days, a bottle of Tylenol, warm baths, and
naps with her heating pad to put her back into operation.

As she lay there one morning with the heating pad,
remembering better days, she suddenly also remembered
that nice, strong young neighbor boy just down the street. His

name was Taylor, or was it Tyler or Thomas? Whatever it was, she knew two things for sure. HER raking days were over and HE was about to come into some money!

I've always preferred happy endings. Don't you?

Chapter 11

Senior Moments Revisited

Some of the Senior Surprises are pretty serious and scary, but somehow it is the simpler senior moments that bother me the most.

I am not sure why. Perhaps it's because they are like the canary in the coal mine: not harmful by itself but a harbinger of what may lie ahead. Or maybe it's because they are more common and more frequent.

Whatever the case, I am a control freak and could not let this go unchallenged. So, it was time to Google my way to the answer.

Of course many studies have been done on how to ward off dementia, or at least slow it down. Most studies have suggestions to try. One thing often mentioned is Make a List or write things down.

When I read that, I thought "I'm home free!" I may be the all-time greatest list maker. I even make lists of my lists. My file cabinet is complete and up to date. My activity calendar is multi-colored to facilitate its use. And, my funeral planner is right there in the top drawer where it will be easy to find.

So why then do I still have trouble remembering some things? More research was needed, so on I continued digging. Having read, researched, cussed and discussed the issue, I can tell you with utmost confidence, NO ONE KNOWS! The only thing to do is stick with my lists and see where it leads.

Yesterday my calendar reminded me it was a Go To Town Day. Time for a list.

1. Library   3 books
2. Pharmacy   Get pill refills, face cream
3. Post Office   Get stamps
4. Grocery store   see list
5. Home   check mailbox

The grocery store list was arranged in the order of the store lay-out, of course. Any coupons were in my purse. My canvas bags were waiting by the door. All was in order.

I made one final trip to the bathroom to "check my lipstick," slipped on my coat, and was out the door and on my way.

It wasn't until I had finished parking in town that I realized I had left my list at home.

Chapter 12

Moment of Truth

Recently after taking a bath, I decided it was time to face the truth. I stood in front of the full-length mirror and just let the towels fall away. Then I took a really good look at what stood before me.

I quickly realized there were two things I must do immediately:

1. Turn the mirror to face the wall.
2. Sit down on the floor and bawl.

Of course, I had known the extra pounds were lurking everywhere: under my chin, under my arms, on my thighs, and around my middle. Who knew that the term "spare tire" could include tractor size? I was mortified and depressed.

My closet full of "this doesn't quite fit any more" clothing had been trying to alert me for months, but I had not listened. Now it was time to take the bull by the horns – or the love handles by the fistfuls – and end this foolishness! Somewhere or somehow, I had to find a plan.

I decided "Do It Yourself" would be my first approach. I already knew the cause: too many calories and not enough exercise. I figured it would be easy to just track my calories taken in daily and see just what I had to deal with. So I did. Again, it was time to sit down – on the bed this time – and bawl. I had learned earlier how hard it was to get back up off the floor!

After wiping my tears, I was ready to determine my exercise level. All I had to do was count my daily steps doing my daily chores.

A chart can be very helpful and show exactly what I needed to know. This was mine:

Area Covered	Number of steps	Repeats
Bedroom to kitchen	30	3 X daily
Bedroom to bath	15	3 X daily
		4 X nightly
Recliner to fridge	8	too many
Office area to fridge	13	3 X daily
Kitchen to basement	40	2 X weekly
House to garage	35	5 X weekly
Trip thru grocery store	300	2 X weekly
Fill birdfeeders	120	3 X weekly
Sweep sidewalk	75	daily

It soon became obvious that it was more complicated than I had thought. I bravely began the calculations. These numbers too, were disheartening. Math has never liked me, nor I it, so it is no wonder the resulting totals were stunning. The conclusion: I WOULD HAVE TO WALK THE DISTANCE OF THE EARTH'S CIRCUMFERENCE AT THE EQUATOR TWO TIMES ON 200 CALORIES A DAY DIET TO REACH MY DESIRED WEIGHT.

But that could be a little off.

So, Plan B is to survey all my friends and ask which weight loss program (they've tried them all) is best and sign up for it right after the holidays.

It would be rude and wasteful to decline all the Christmas goodies friends and neighbors so eagerly offer, don't you think?

Chapter 13

Fingernails

Who ever imagined that fingernails would become a senior surprise? Not me, yet it was so. All my life I have been a nail biter. . . For years my family bombarded me daily with lectures and every birthday and Christmas with manicure sets, to no avail. They finally just gave up and let me gnaw at will.

As I got older, I got better and learned to just nibble my thumbnail surreptitiously in public. Then much later, I developed bone issues and the doctor prescribed a twice-a-year shot to strengthen my bones.

I'm not sure how it affected my bones, but my nails were growing at warp speed with space-age hardness. A family of beavers could not handle the cutting. I got so desperate I bought my own manicure set. It was too late. Small scissor loops did not fit over swollen knuckles and the clipper took more strength than old joints could muster. After a lifetime of neglect, my nails were getting their revenge. I could not blame them.

But the problems remained. What choices did I have? It was either find a farrier or make an appointment with the pedicurist shop in the mall. Their ad said it all:

NEED A PEDICURE?

CALL: get-toe-trim

Even I can manage that! Wish me luck.

Chapter 14

The Hanky

Some people are said to be born with a silver spoon in their mouth. I was not one of them, but I swear I WAS born with a large size, white, men's handkerchief in my hand. One has been there every day since.

I don't know where that hanky came from, but it was just what an allergy-ridden, "environmentally sensitive," drippy-nosed kid needed to get through the day. Eighty-plus years later, as long as I have that hanky at my side, or up my sleeve, or tucked into my belt, or in my pocket or under my pillow, I am ready to take on the world.

There were challenges along the way, but my mother helped. Years ago, Monday was designated wash day and washing was hung outdoors to dry. Honest. Our clothesline included more square feet of hankies than anyone in town, hands down. Ironing came next. After dampening the cloth and letting it sit a bit, one ironed them and carefully folded them for storage. They were my responsibility and my introduction to Domestic Bliss, 101. Easy peasy.

But things in life change. My simple drippy-nose dilemma became a more serious respiratory issue. Before I knew it, shortness of breath was limiting my ability to do the things I had always taken for granted. It was scary, and serious help was required.

Life "with hanky" was not always fun or easy, but life with full-time oxygen use could truly stop me in my tracks. It was a major reality check for me.

The facts were clear. I needed help and oxygen was the answer. I became depressed, withdrawn, disheartened and angry. All very understandable. It was a familiar life scenario. First you mope, then you cope.

Several weeks of what I called my "air conditioning period" introduced me to what I could expect "living on air," so to speak.

Clumsy moments dodging the air hose; countless minutes dealing with air hose; occasional need to replace air hose; reluctant occasions in public with air hose; much wasted breath cursing air hose; futile efforts distracting cat from air hose. Who ever imagined "air hose" would be the most hated and most feared phrase in the English language?

But any word or phrase repeated enough in rapid succession soon loses its meaning and its relevance. Common sense again prevails and sets you free!

Thus, you gather 30 feet of hose in one hand and your cane in the other and go trippingly on your way to the next surprise. As you surely have guessed by now, surprises never end.

Chapter 15

The Fall

Did I really say "trippingly?" Dear Lord, my mind is truly gone. Talk about red flags and mad bulls, I better start looking for a soft place to land!

But it was too late, of course. That very day at 7:04 p.m. my two sets of air hoses snarled themselves around my ankles and dumped me face first against the wall. I landed on both forearms, bumped my head on the wall, and knew I was in trouble.

At 3:15 a.m. my family escorted me back home from the E.R., broken right (WRONG) wrist in a temporary cast until I met with the orthopedist the next day. Her verdict: double fracture, no complications, 6 weeks in a cast.

Back at home, every safety measure was belatedly taken. Automatic night lights were installed everywhere, all loose rugs were relegated to the dog house, sturdy footwear was laced up tight and an order for a medical alert pendant was on its way. All was done to assure as much peace of mind as any of us would ever have again.

Through it all, not one harsh word was spoken, at least not out loud.

That was not the surprise. To learn that, please read on.

Lessons Learned

Tripped and fell,
Broke my wrist.
Can't do much
Here's the list:

Can't wash my face
Or brush my hair.
Lashes, lips and cheeks
Are bare.

Cannot brush my teeth
Or floss.
Stinky breath
Will make one cross.

Kitchen chores?
I'm at a loss;
Good thing I don't
Have a boss.

Open jar, pop or cap?
Someone else can handle that.
Slice, dice or fricassee?
All of them are beyond me.

Try to use
A broom or mop.
The mess just grows
So I just stop.

No email, texts,
Computer games
To take up time
And ease the pain.

Cannot button
Cannot tie,
Tuck a shirt in
Though I try.

Can't wipe my butt
Or sink a putt
Can't shake a hand
Or crack a nut.

When everything
Is done and said
Next time I'm landing
On my head.

Just Another Senior Surprise

Chapter 16

The Christmas Letter

It is said that the devil finds work of idle hands. Few hands are more idle than mine lately and I am more than happy to give the devil his due for the project I found myself struggling with in early December.

FROM SOMEWHERE I got the notion to write my own Christmas letter to family and friends. This was precipitated by my totally inexplicable finding of some pretty Christmas stationery in a kitchen drawer. The paper was 9 x 11 with a birchbark look and edged with green pine boughs, red ribbons and holly leaves; very festive, but not gaudy.

It was only later that I realized how thoroughly I'd been suckered in. This "magic find" gave me a chance to:

A. Waste not;
B. Be creative and personal;
C. Save money by not having to "buy anything!"

My spirit soared. (The devil smiled.)
Everything you do as a senior is a serious struggle. It

takes longer, tests your abilities and resolve, and turns out to be less than you hoped for or intended. But you carry on. Before long I had my message ready. I wanted it to be simple, informative, warm and sincere and it was. Part 1 was done.

Part 2 would transfer my message to a master copy which would be reproduced by my FAX machine, inserted into addressed envelopes and sent on its way. I smiled. (The devil giggled.)

My typewriter is old, seldom used, never maintained and full of dust, dirt, eraser chaff and cookie crumbs, but it is at least electric. However, it wasn't typing clearly or cleanly. The letter wheel was dirty and out of alignment. I had no idea how to fix that. Good old German bullheadedness would have to carry me through the challenge once more. Two days later with the sacrifice of many hours and my personal toothbrush, I got the wheel cleaned and printing properly.

It turned out that the devil was not the only one helping me with my project. Murphy and his Law were right there beside him. I had no idea what the phrase "Anything that can go wrong, will go wrong" might include. Turns out, it was a lot. It was the correction tape that failed me next.

It took some deep digging through desk drawers and cupboards to finally find a set of those slippery devils. You DO NOT want to drop either of those snarly reels, but I did, of course. Nonetheless, I was finally actually able to produce some readable print. Amazing.

Many wasted pages of stationery later I finally had a master copy to try in my printer. I carefully loaded the paper tray, inserted my copy, checked all the possible options, and pushed START. Sure enough, a copy emerged. Clear, neat, and on the wrong side of the stationery. (Some chuckling was heard; not mine.)

I refilled the paper tray, took a deep breath, and again hit START. Three loud BEEPS sounded and a message appeared in the message box. My magenta was empty. Say, what?? I soon learned one ink cartridge was empty and no printing would happen without it. That would require a trip to town and I'm no longer a driver. I admit it. I cried.

Two days later my nerves were calmed as my elves had brought me a new set of ink cartridges and a new toothbrush. The final push began. I glanced at the calendar. December 12th. It was now or never for my project to succeed. I had addressed the envelopes so only the message was left to print. I hit START for what I prayed would be the final time, and waited.

Slowly but surely 20 neatly printed pages piled up on the desk before me. They were perfect. Or, as we seniors often must say, "close enough!"

I sighed in relief and just shut my eyes and stood quietly for a prayerful moment. Then, just as I looked up, I swear I caught a glimpse of two thumbs up hovering in the distance.

All I could say was, "Merry Christmas, guys! I couldn't have done it without you!"

Just Another Senior Surprise

Chapter 17

Dr. I. C. Red

Of course, I know better than to make any appointments for a Monday. Today's appointment was proof positive it was a bad idea, and should never be done again. And it won't. At least not by me. I can't speak for "them", WHO MADE THIS APPOINTMENT FOR ME.

It all started because I have been having some eye problems for some time. While reading, my vision may blur, focus come and go, and my eyes burn and tear. Reading is hard or impossible, and reading is my biggest joy in life. Not reading is not living. I needed a cure.

Thus, an appointment with my long-time local optometrist was first. He said, "I think you have developed secondary cataracts, a common occurrence after cataract surgery, usually occurring four or five years later. These can be easily removed by laser. The process is short and simple, takes fifteen minutes, is outpatient and fully covered by insurance. It can be done in Bemidji, only an hour away." Of course, I went for it. His office set it up.

My appointment was set for today at 11 a.m. at the

43

new medical center in Bemidji. I had never been there. BUT WAIT!

The story really starts yesterday.....

Sunday

I have barely been out of the house since Christmas. I have no clothes fit to be worn in public (due to assorted reasons and excess pounds), can't go anywhere without full oxygen supply and related paraphernalia guaranteeing me a safe trip, and have a grumpy gut that tends to "fire at will" whether Will is ready or not. This requires me to be cognizant of any and all toilet facilities at all times. So, no, going out is not my favorite thing to do.

I had finally managed to work out these concerns enough to consider it all a "GO." This meant an alarm clock would be involved. So what, you ask? For reasons unknown and apparently unsolvable, setting an alarm is just not in my capabilities range. I invariably lie awake most of the night clock-watching so I don't miss the sound of the alarm, whether it is set right or not. Dumb, but true and incurable. This night I set it right and at 7 a.m. the screeching beeper began its aggravating call as I watched the digits drop on the clock's face. I got up, sleep deprived, but ready for the day. Or so I hoped.

We arrived at the clinic in good shape. It turned out to be a large sprawling collection of concrete blocks, red stonework and endless parking areas, none of which were

44

anywhere near a door. It was located by three major highways all going nowhere anyone wanted to go: Red Lake, Winnipeg, International Falls, plus the Twin Cities.

There was not one pleasant or appealing thing about any of it. Inside the "Welcome" motif continued. Endless beige carpet, or brown, black and gray carpet tiles covered everything, including some walls. I immediately wanted to bang my head on one. Long halls to nowhere, endless area markers or direction arrows – Children, Eyes, Cardiac – clearly told everyone where to go. I sorely wanted to return the favor.

It was all under the control – or at least observation of, endless people clad in ill-fitting garments of tan, brown or grey, and none were in the least bit stylish. None, God and all the saints forbid, were COLORFUL! It was depressing.

After two trips to inspect the plumbing and one to change the air supply battery, I met my first "professional." She took us to an exam room and began her inquisition. Juli was seated by her side at the desk trying to run interference and trying to keep my hearing loss up to date amid all the gibberish coming my way. Juli is my daughter-in-law and thankfully willing to be my guide and driver for health-related appointments. She has had some medical training and experience and does not hesitate to speak up or ask questions. I call her my personal Sherpa guide. Climbing Mt. Everest is a walk in the park compared to getting old.

The questions went from "Date of birth?" all the way to the ever popular but understated "Do you ever wish you were dead?" I was really tempted with that one, but managed to settle for a simple "no" as the reply.

Next came the eye exam and questions. None of it made any sense to me. Juli had been reading over her shoulder and finally said, "' I think you have the wrong paper work there. It should be for Karen Dyre, but this says Karen J_____ on it".

The lady replies "It's a good thing you noticed that." She gets my vote for the professional error recovery of the year.

Thus began part two of the inquisition. By the time she got to "Do you drink?" all I could possibly say was, "No but I'm thinking of starting soon."

We were soon released to the waiting area where the doctor would "see us soon."

FYI: "soon" is a relative concept but it <u>will</u> eventually occur. With it this time came a 40ish, red-haired and skimpy-bearded guy in a pink shirt, no tie. He signaled me to enter the room, followed by Juli with all our survival gear. Red never introduced himself in any way, never welcomed us, never indicated any interest in or concern with my problem, and was obviously late for lunch. By now who wasn't?

He spoke only to Juli, and they determined after viewing my eye exam reports that I did not need laser surgery, but would do fine with up-dated lenses. New frames would be optional: my choice.

He finally turned to me and said, "You could take some lutein every day. It keeps eyes healthy and only costs $30 per month. You don't have to though."

Do they make greeting cards that say:

THANKS FOR NOTHING,
YOU JERK!

There is surely a need. I must contact Hallmark and find out.

By this time, I was just about out of oxygen and totally out of patience, but managed to keep my mouth shut and eyes closed till we got to the car. No one had even offered me a sunshield for my eyes. We both sat in the car, exhausted and wondering just what we'd accomplished by our trip. No ready answer came to mind. Nor did the debacle come to an end.

I went the next day to the optometrist to order the new lenses and frames. It would take 7-10 days, so I waited. Then a call said they were here. Before I could even react, a second call told me they sent the wrong ones. Another week was likely, but they would call.

I was about ready to start interviewing seeing-eye dogs when someone finally set new glasses on my nose and sent me on my way to the pile of new books awaiting me next to my favorite chair. So many books; so little time!

Would someone please bring me a Pepsi?

Thanks everyone . . . except you, Red!

Chapter 18

The Bucket List

People talk a lot about their "bucket list." Would you like some advice? Go for it! Whether it's April in Paris, Fantasy with Disney, a Corn Hole contest in Kansas or a wild ride to Hog Heaven in Sturgis, do it NOW! Your chance can be gone in a second and you'll end up like the rest of us, empty-handed and chagrined.

By the time you reach your eighties any list you have left will barely cover the bottom of a child's sand bucket. All grandiose plans will have withered, all wild notions have been tamed.

Serious life changes can occur at any time too. For example, a good friend recently moved to her daughter's home in another town, a common move for seniors of a certain age and condition. We have become ardent pen pals and include the postal service in our nightly prayers. It is our last hope for private sharing.

My friend's recent letter could well be a bucket list for seniors. She listed all the things she wished for daily: being able to put curlers in her own hair, cut her own nails, button any button, scrub her own back, put on the winter jacket and

49

boots without help. It was a familiar list. How easily it could become yours!

That should be reason enough to take action. Buy that plane ticket! Make those reservations! Choose Powerball numbers! Just do it!

You can't win if you don't play. Give the Wheel of Fortune a spin . . . Pat and Vanna would wish you well.

And so do I.

Chapter 19

Dreams

Dreams have always fascinated me. What do they mean? Where do they come from? Why THIS dream NOW? How should I treat them? I have never come up with an answer and as far as I can determine, neither has anyone else.

As if that wasn't enough to ponder, I noticed that the senior dream world was a whole different place. Suddenly I find myself more at risk in early morning. I awaken about 4 a.m. or so, fall back to sleep, and am immediately engulfed in dreams.

These extravaganzas are unlike anything in my usual dreams. They are more wild and frightening than a double feature movie by Frederico Fellini and the Coen brothers on drugs. And they go on and on and on.

If I am jolted awake, then fall back to sleep again, the dream is right there waiting for me. I have my own to-be-continued soap opera just waiting for me and I am helpless.

But stranger still, I can hardly wait for bedtime so I can see what the dream world has to offer next.

Few things are as boring as listening to someone else's

dream description, so I will spare you that. I just thought you may wish to save a spot for "Dreams" on your Senior Surprise Roster of Coming Events. They <u>are</u> coming.

Trust me.

FYI: If I am reading a book and fall asleep, the Dream Master takes over and I just continue the story in my sleep. Would that be plagiarism?

Chapter 20

Music of the Night

I don't believe I've mentioned the night music yet. It arrived again last night just as it had several times before. I was lying in bed all cuddled up and warm, ready for a good night's sleep and I barely noticed the music at first. It was very soft but compelling, a full orchestral offering I could not identify. Calm, but persistent, it played on.

There was no turning it off, of course. No volume control. It just went on playing its tune. We've all had times when certain songs or jingles keep running through our heads, but this was a whole different thing. I began to wonder about it.

The first five years of my life we lived in a small apartment house. It was a place that surrounded you with the lives of other people. You recognized their footsteps on the stairs, heard their conversations through the walls, and smelled their cooking everywhere. This night music reminded me of those years. It seemed old, yet new; presumably shared, not owned. Persistent but not over-powering. Was it a remembrance or a premonition? I did not know.

In those early years our entertainment was the radio.

53

This music seemed an echo of those days. Then suddenly the orchestra stopped playing. In the background I could plainly hear the strains of "Auld Lang Syne." An old acquaintance most surely "not forgot!"

But this was not just any "Auld Lang Syne." This was the classic version played by Guy Lombardo and his Royal Canadians Orchestra every New Year's Eve from New York City at the stroke of midnight. "The sweetest music this side of heaven!" And its slow tempo, wailing saxophones, and deep beat were unmistakable. It took me back to long ago and far away in a four count.

But what did it mean here and now? Was it new or old? Good or bad? Remembrance or warning? I had no idea but no way could I let it rest. There are certain forces that you simply can't ignore.

I threw on my robe and headed for my desk where my computer, Mr.-Know-It-All, awaited my command. But of course, even a computer needs your question before it can offer an answer. Let's face it. Three a.m. is not my very best problem-solving time. Perhaps a good night's sleep will fortify my mental acuity for what could be an extensive search for truth and clarity in the reasons for this music of the night.

Let's see . . . There will be lots of topics to research . . . music, Andrew Lloyd Weber, New Years celebrations, winter nights, apartment living, memories, mental illness.

I promise, you'll be the second to know. Meanwhile, could you turn off the light, please?

Chapter 21

Bored

I'm bored. Bored, bored, bored, bored, bored. No surprise there. When you live in a one mule town – they couldn't afford a horse! - bored is what you get. The only way this town will ever have a really HOT time is if it burns down. Even I don't wish for that.

It wouldn't be so bad if you could at least depend on your best friend Lucy to call every day like she promised to do, but never does. Or claims she called but I just didn't hear the phone ring. Well, I must admit that <u>has</u> happened.

I need to know if she is going to church on Sunday and what she is going to wear. It seems almost sacrilegious what people wear to church these days. Our mothers would have been totally mortified if we had shown up anywhere with torn jeans, holey t-shirts, exposed bra straps and flipflops, to say nothing of creepy tattoos crawling up every part of your body. If you do dress decently, they think YOU are a freak or an old-fashioned fool! Well, I make no apologies when I'm right.

Lucy was supposed to call me with the name of the new face cream product she read about in a magazine she saw at the Senior Center. It is supposed to "reduce wrinkles, soften skin, tighten drooping and bring back your natural glow." I hope it comes in the large economy size.

Maybe they'll have something to kill all the nose and chin hairs that have replaced acne as the number one enemy on the beauty front. Lucy and I get together when we can and have a plucking party to see how many of those pesky things we can eliminate. It's an endless and painful process.

I did see a woman in town one day who had a full grown, neatly trimmed mustache quivering over her trembling upper lip. Brave, but not trendy. I have learned the wisdom of "never say never."

So, I am back to bored. I guess I will just continue to sleep till noon to shorten my day, sit by the phone in case Lucy calls, and try to figure out a project to fill my day.

I wonder if it's time to bring back macrame.

Chapter 22

Music Out of Tune

Earlier I told you about my "Music of the Night," including Guy Lombardo's "Auld Lang Syne." It was an interesting musical interlude I truly enjoyed and I was sorry it suddenly ended its visits.

I will never say that about the musical mess that replaced it. This is music in a whole different key. I call it "The Intruder" and I dread it daily.

It is insistent, inconsiderate, annoying and musically flat. It will intrude on phone calls, naps, reading times, or personal visits without a qualm. Its only limitations seem to be that it must appear about on the half-hour only. It seems to favor 10:30, but any :30 is fair game. That's also 24/7, 7/7, 12/12, apparently ad infinitum.

My hearing issues have kept the volume low enough so it has not driven me quite round the bend just yet. But I do hear enough to know I have had enough. So, what do I do to end it?

You are probably wondering how I have come to this desperate state and dubious as to how music could have brought me there. I am hesitant to explain it, in fear that it could set YOU up for a similar state of mind. The power of suggestion is a formidable foe and music is insidious by nature. YOU could be at risk.

With that disclaimer, here are the tunes that complete my maddening musicale:

1. Good King Wenceslas (Christmas carol)
2. The Wheels on the Bus Go Round and Round
3. 99 Bottles of Beer on the Wall

My case rests.

Chapter 23

Déjà vu

Remember that day during a super cold Minnesota winter when you were a stay-at-home Mom with 2½ preschoolers and a crazy 6-month-old Labrador retriever puppy that your usually sensible hunting-addicted husband had brought home last summer? You looked out the window and realized the sun was shining, no wind was blowing, and the January thaw they had been promising had kicked the temperature up to 45 degrees. The eaves were dripping on the new red sled Santa had brought which was leaning against the garage wall waiting to be played with. You decided it was time for everyone to get some fresh air, so you started to gather up boots and jackets and mittens and caps. This sent the pup into a frenzy because he knew jacket meant "out" and he was more than ready to play in the snow. Then you started tucking wiggly bodies into soft bundles, wondering where your own mittens might be, but finally got everyone lined up by the front door. You were just reaching for the door knob when you heard a soft voice say, "Mommy, I need to pee!"

It will all come back to you again on some future winter day when you have happily spent the morning picking out a nice casual outfit, fussing a bit with make-up and hair, and gift-wrapping those pretty silver earrings as a gift for your good friend's 80th Valentine's Day birthday which you will celebrate with friends in town.

The memory will return at the exact moment you carefully make your way down the steps to the garage, take a seat in the car, start the engine and let it warm up a bit as you press the garage door opener. You settle your purse and the gift on the seat beside you, tighten your seat-belt and finally reach for the gear shift lever.

That's when you will hear for the first time, but not the last time, those famous words.

"I need to pee."

But this time they will be yours.

Chapter 24

Multi-tasking

My mother would be the first to tell you, doing my chores was never a reward-winning event in our home. Oh, I would eventually get the dishes wiped and put away. My bed was made most days. On laundry day I could be expected to do my share. It was just never any truly special event.

That's why I have been so surprised at my success with this new concept, multi-tasking. I have to tell you, folks, I AM KILLING IT!!

Somewhere, somehow, I have developed a superior knack for combining many talents and tasks for maximum results. Here's a recent example.

It was lunch time and a trip to the fridge had little to offer except a couple of slices of ham and a little left-over potato salad. I decided that should fill the plate and my stomach as well. It would have to, except I just happened to knock over a small pitcher of ice water I keep on the top shelf.

Mother would also say you never know how much water a glass holds until you spill it. It can be quite a lot. In this case, it managed to douse two glass shelves, trickle into one vegetable crisper, splash over 3 door shelves and the many small items therein, then drip onto the kitchen floor and slide under the refrigerator out of sight.

Paper toweling grabbed the first puddles, as I moved all items to the kitchen counters. It would take more than that to dry things off, so I headed to the linen closet for more towels. That's where I came upon distraction # 1.

I had a new cleaning lady do the laundry that week and the linen closet was a mess. I gave it a quick shuffle and re-do and was back in the kitchen in 10 minutes with fresh towels to finish the job.

That took some serious time. I sifted, sorted and threw away many things, then dried off the rest and arranged them in sensible order on the shelves. It had needed my attention.

The floor was next. A quick move of the fridge turned up another neglected area. Dust, crumbs, bugs and cobwebs awaited me. They, too, were soon gone. All that remained was a quick mop job for the floor.

I forced myself to check the dining area floor next to the kitchen. A mopping was needed there, too. And I might as well shake out the area rugs in the hall and vacuum the carpet. I grabbed the vacuum, turned it on, and realized it was not picking anything up. The bag was full. Distraction # 2.

This sent me to the "cupboard from hell." Re-doing it would take all day, so I dug down far enough to find a new bag, changed it out, and went back to finishing the floors. It was now nearly 2 p.m.

As a rule, senior citizens are as flexible as the rest

of the world, but some things in our lives are simply non-negotiable. At the top of that list is Nap Time.

Nap time choices can vary from 12:30 to 3 p.m. My preference was more in the middle of that spread but today 2 p.m. sounded just right. I was tired.

You must admit it, it was a record-breaking run. Perhaps a personal best. Whatever the case, it was time for me to put the mop away, grab two cookies and a glass of milk, and head for my napping chair. The snuggly blanket awaited me.

I had definitely reached The End.

And so have you.

Just Another Senior Surprise

Chapter 25

The Telephone

I'm sure Alexander Graham Bell meant well. He was just a simple scientist and engineer who wanted to understand how things worked and perhaps make them better for everyone's use. He did that with his telephone in 1876.

Have you ever noticed how it is never the prime inventor who causes any problems? It's always the "tweakers." Those busy-bodies can never just leave well enough alone. They are the cause of all the complications and "improvement" that the rest of us struggle with day to day, especially if you are a "senior." (You may be able to teach some old dogs new tricks, but don't bet too much money on their remembering them for long.)

Which brings us back to the telephone. First there were numbers. One summer my phone number was the single digit #7. In no time it grew to 3589-LW. I clearly recall "party lines" which had nothing to do with politics and "double rings" which in no way included weddings.

Live operators originally placed your call for you. These ladies were all-knowing, generally pleasant and helpful, spoke only English and without accent. Good old days, indeed.

Today's phones are a study in over-kill and totally unnecessary for the average bear....or human. They are universally despised by any normal senior who is affronted by being made to feel like a fool every time he touches a phone. Their size is anathema to any usefulness.

The work surface is crammed full of numbers, letters, and daunting choices and pitfalls of all kinds. The buttons are difficult for anyone to hit, and all but impossible for someone with arthritic joints or challenging tremors. It's disrespectful and embarrassing. The excessiveness of it all makes for a slow and confusing process. Any accidental bump or touch can send it all crashing into never-to-be-seen again country. A good place for it.

Frustration abounds. Hard to hold, hard to hear, hard to operate, hard to tolerate, it surely is not Mr. Edison's finest functioning telephone any more. We're sorry sir. Very, very, very, very, sorry. Indeed!

Chapter 26

The Computer Class

My struggle with the cell phone was annoying, but not nearly
as bad as the computer challenge. That battle started over
10 years ago and I was already 10 years behind. It was idle
hands and simple curiosity that led me there, never a good
combination. Before I knew it, I was seated at a desk in Room
107 of the local high school, all signed in for my first adult
education class, Intro to Computers.

I was not alone. Twelve others had chosen Monday
night from 7 to 9:30 pm. for honing our skills and setting the
bar for all classes to follow. My first thought was, "Thirteen is
not a fortuitous number."

I recognized some of them: a local dairy farmer
who would have lots of records to keep, a legal secretary
"keeping current," some younger guys wishing they'd paid
more attention in their keyboarding class in high school, and
a few seniors like me. We had all seen the handwriting on
the wall, or in this case on the blackboard, and it plainly said
"Computers are here to stay. Are you?"

I suddenly realized I was sitting on my chair with both

hands tightly tucked under my thighs and nowhere near the keyboard. This seemed a little counter-productive to me, so I loosened my hands, gave them a shake and tentatively "stroked "a key. We had been told one NEVER hits, strikes or jabs a computer key. You "stroke" it. My cat probably would take offense at this intrusion into his territory, but rules are rules. I spent the next several minutes stroking the keys until I thought I may "stroke out" myself. It didn't help, but I struggled on.

It was finally break time and the instructor told us the next thing we'd tackle would be the spreadsheet. That did it. The only spread sheet of interest to me was the one on my bed at home, where I would much rather be. I had already sat there for over an hour, totally deluged in a torrent of terms and directions that were so foreign to me I thought I may have accidentally stumbled into the classroom where they were offering lessons in Finnish 101. It had been listed in the fall brochure, too. As it turned out, it really was my "Finnish" class. I had had enough.

I tried to explain this to the instructor in a nice way, and he gave me no argument, just said I was welcome to return any time and wished me well. A true gentleman.

Being a quitter has never been my style though, and pride still goeth before the fall, so I bit the bullet, bought my own laptop computer and found a large instructional manual I still refer to as my Finnish dictionary.

I thereby became the most annoying mortal in a 5-mile radius. Friends, neighbors and total strangers soon flinched at the sight of me. There was no escaping my neediness.

Make no mistake. These are not bad or heartless people. They just have problems of their own and frankly don't care just where my lost email goes. I totally understand and forgive them. But I still need help.

If anyone out there can help, call soon. The cat and I are waiting, though he is starting to lose interest somehow. Cats will be cats.

Just Another Senior Surprise

Chapter 27

The Challenge

I recently had the experience of not only recalling the phrase "a day late and a dollar short," but also getting to experience it, in spades! Let me explain.

You all know my limitations in the world of technology. I do recognize its astounding capabilities and endless possibilities, but still think there's a way to make it all more user friendly for seniors. Sometimes in life, less is more.

I decided it was time to throw out a challenge for all would-be entrepreneurs of the world to solve this problem once and for all.

I decided a nice poster would be an easy way to present the challenge. It would need to be short, simple, specific, and guarantee sure compensation later. A copy is attached.

Next, I needed to state exactly what we needed for senior use. That took several days of thought and paper wasting and was more complicated than I imagined, but I scribbled on. It was a good waste of February in Minnesota.

Things had finally come together and I decided to close my plea with a short poem to inspire the challengers.

It filled the page nicely, made good sense, and ended my presentation. All that was left was to call the printer and check into costs and timetable. The end was near, I decided. Never had I been so right.

At that very moment I heard the familiar thunk of the mail dropping into my mailbox on the door. The delivery included the usual newspaper, three letters seeking donations, two catalogs, and a letter from a good friend and long-time pen pal.

I opened her letter and found the usual report on health issues, family doings, general comments on life, PLUS a small brochure/insert that had no doubt been included in one of her recent magazines.

IT WAS AN ADVERTISEMENT FOR A BRAND NEW, JUST ON THE MARKET, SIMPLIFIED COMPUTER FOR SENIORS. It was also temporarily being offered at a $200 discount for only $1,000.

Even in my diminished senior capacities, I clearly understood my situation. I was many months late and $999.00 short.

ATTENTION

Would-be

ENTREPRENEURS

A CHALLENGE AWAITS!

Simplify technology for seniors!

Make it easy, make it fast, make it now

40 MILLION SENIOR CITIZENS ARE
AWAITING YOUR PRODUCT

JUST REMEMBER
If in life you would succeed
First of all, define a need.
Meet that need, and I am told,
Your pockets will be filled with gold. *

Ready, Set, Simplify!

*Harvey McKay could not have said it better!

Chapter 28

Shopping Online

Speaking of things I know nothing about, be sure to include online shopping. I avoided it as long as I could, but it was the weatherman who pushed me over the edge into debatable buying practices.

His predictions in March promised "much above normal temperatures" for the summer with dry, windy conditions as well. Seemed like the perfect time to give computer shopping a try.

I needed some new summer clothes, preferably cool, casual dresses reasonably priced and comfortable to wear. Could the computer help? Boy, could it! In no time at all I was up to my neck in apparel choices from around the world. I decided on an ad showing attractive models in simple colorful frocks, attractively displayed in summery settings. I made choices, sent my order, sat back and waited. It was June 3rd.

I planned to wear the red dress I picked for a 4th of July outing. Another dress was my favorite shade of blue. The 3rd was a shade of gold with a flowered pattern. Summery for sure.

July 4th came. The red dress did not. I began to wonder

if I should re-check my order. I quickly discovered the company was in fact "licensed in the United Kingdom." Never mind a phone call. I waited.

August arrived, and I decided the company must be some type of cooperative that merchandised items from various new designers, pooling their products to get them to market. A sensible plan, I thought, so I waited.

It was August 14th when my package finally arrived, coming as it turned out, all the way from CHINA! I quickly gathered my friends for the grand opening. Excitement reigned.

I opened the red dress first. It was a simple pull-over style with side seam pockets, tiny white hearts for a pattern, on silky fabric. It would work just fine.

The blue dress was similar but in slip-cut style. The fabric again was slippery and shiny with a paisley – style pattern. It would do for a nightie, if nothing else.

The third dress was not "the charm." It was a shade of yellow that only a hot dog should ever wear. The fabric's splashes of flowery swirls did nothing to enhance or obliterate the yellow. On top of that, it was so sheer only an exotic dancer would dare to wear it. A sleeveless scoop-necked top was clumsily attached to a very full skirt so long that even stiletto heels would not get it off the floor. That would take stilts . . . or a very sharp scissors.

I have my faults and short-comings, but no one has ever accused me of being a slow learner. I know when I'm whipped! I wasted no more time even trying them on. The local thrift shop perhaps could find them a home. I was done with them. All that was left for me to do was mark it all up to Life Lesson Learned #19,834 and counting.

Just Another Senior Surprise

Chapter 29

Final Thoughts

There are a lot of every day concerns that hang over your head as you await the next Senior Surprise. Most of them run through your mind between 1 and 3 a.m. as you toss in bed hoping those leg cramps will let up soon.

This is when you think about all the changes in your life and try to decide which ones really matter. For example, I can deal with the wrinkles adorning my once smooth and rosy cheeks: both sets. If my "Five foot two, eyes of blue" status is now "4' 11" and "cataract corrected," so be it. As for the hearing loss, no one can carry on a decent conversation any more anyway. What you can't alter, you may as well accept gracefully and move on.

So, there you have it, the tale of the Senior Surprises. Other episodes will surely be added to the list in time. Perhaps someone else will see fit to tell their tale. For me, for now, this is enough to share with those in their 60's to 80's who are brave enough to research what lies ahead.

Do I have any advice to offer? Only this: you can panic, pout or persevere: the choice is yours. Just remember to keep your sense of humor close by and know that you are not alone.

I expect Senior Surprises will go on and on until the end, and that will be the biggest surprise of all.

Chapter 30

The Final Call

My treatise has tried to guide you through the mental mine-field of aging with wisdom and patience and a bit of humor from time to time. Now here we are, just a few steps away from the very last set of instructions.

Of course I don't have the actual experience to aid you. All I know for sure is, it is always best to "be prepared." With that in mind, I offer the following things to think about as you await the final call.

Personal Agenda
On arriving at the Pearly Gates or:
The Pearly Protocol

1. **Call first, or just show up?**
2. **Shoes, or no shoes?**
3. **Proper first contact?**
   Shake hands
   Bump Elbows
   Kneel humbly

4. **Vocal greeting?**
   "Saint Peter, I presume?"
   "I'm honored, your Holiness"
   "Yo, Bro!"

5. **Next Step?**
   Enter and isolate for 2 weeks
   (COVID-19 Protocol in 2020)
   Enter and await instructions
   Enter and "Party on!"

6. **Identification required?**
   Obituary copy
   AARP membership card
   Latest dental records

7. **Certificate of Entitlement?**
   Death certificate
   Funeral bill marked 'Paid in Full'
   Note from Pastor and 3 close friends

8. **Food and Shelter?**
   Package deal
   Optional choices (See brochure)

9. **Contact Family and Friends?**
   Look for cardboard sign with your name
   Try email

10. **Sign up for classes/activities?**
    Harp playing
    Chariot Racing
    Flying lessons

11. **Volunteer for Duty?**

    Cloud fluffing

    Gate polishing

    Apple harvest

12. **Final Step?**

    Give Thanks

    Relax

    Enjoy!

Made in the USA
Monee, IL
14 October 2021

79960402R10056